NOBLE BEASTS

NATIONAL GALLERY OF ART

NOBLE BEASTS

Animals in Art

COMPILED AND EDITED BY BRIAN D. HOTCHKISS

A BULFINCH PRESS BOOK ✢ LITTLE, BROWN AND COMPANY

BOSTON ✢ NEW YORK ✢ TORONTO ✢ LONDON

ENDPAPERS: Circle of Jan van Kessel, *Study of Birds and Monkeys*, 1660/1670
BAS-TITLE: Edward Hicks, *Peaceable Kingdom* (detail), c. 1834
FRONTISPIECE: Sir Peter Paul Rubens, *Lion*, c. 1614

FIRST EDITION

Library of Congress Cataloging-in-Publication Data

National Gallery of Art (U.S.)
    Noble beasts: animals in art / National Gallery of Art; compiled and edited by
Brian D. Hotchkiss. — 1st ed.
        p.   cm.
    "A Bulfinch Press book."
    Includes index.
    ISBN 0-8212-2109-4
    1. Animals in art — Catalogs.   2. Animals, Mythical, in art — Catalogs.   3. Animals —
Literary collections.   4. Art — Washington (D.C.) — Catalogs.   5. National Gallery of Art
(U.S.) — Catalogs.   I. Hotchkiss, Brian D.   II. Title.
N7662.N38   1994
704.9'432'074753 — dc20   94-4651

Bulfinch Press is an imprint and trademark of Little, Brown and Company (Inc.)
Published simultaneously in Canada by Little, Brown & Company (Canada) Limited

PRINTED IN ITALY

Contents

The Creation of the Animals

The sixth, and of creation last arose
With evening harps and matin, when God said,
Let the earth bring forth soul living in her kind,
Cattle and creeping things, and beast of the earth,
Each in their kind. The earth obeyed, and straight
Opening her fertile womb teemed at a birth
Innumerous living creatures, perfect forms,
Limbed and full grown: out of the ground up rose
As from his lair the wild beast where he wons
In forest wild, in thicket, brake, or den;
Among the trees in pairs they rose, they walked:
The cattle in the fields and meadows green:
Those rare and solitary, these in flocks
Pasturing at once, and in broad herds upsprung.
The grassy clods now calved, now half appeared
The tawny lion, pawing to get free
His hinder parts, then springs as broke from bonds,
And rampant shakes his brinded mane; the ounce,
The libbard, and the tiger, as the mole
Rising, the crumbled earth above them threw
In hillocks; the swift stag from underground
Bore up his branching head: scarce from his mould
Behemoth biggest born of earth upheaved
His vastness: fleeced the flocks and bleating rose,
As plants: ambiguous between sea and land
The river horse and scaly crocodile.

JOHN MILTON, 1608–1674 FROM *Paradise Lost*

ATTRIBUTED TO JAN VAN KESSEL, *Concert of Birds*, 1660/1670

I

from Arctic Dreams

The polar bear is a creature of arctic edges: he hunts the ice margins, the surface of the water, and the continental shore. The ice bear, he is called. His world forms beneath him in the days of shortening light, and then falls away in the spring. He dives to the ocean floor for mussels and kelp, and soundlessly breaks the water's glassy surface on his return, to study a sleeping seal. Twenty miles from shore he treads water amid schooling fish. The sea bear. In winter, while the grizzly hibernates, the polar bear is out on the sea ice, hunting. In summer his tracks turn up a hundred miles inland, where he has feasted on crowberries and blueberries. . . .

What was so impressive about the bear we saw that day in the Chukchi was how robust he seemed. At three years of age a bear in this part of the Arctic is likely spending its first summer alone. To feed itself, it has had to learn to hunt, and open pack ice is among the toughest of environments for bears to hunt in. This was September, when most bears are thin, waiting for the formation of sea ice, their hunting platform. In our three days of diligent searching, in this gray and almost featureless landscape of ice remnants so far off the coast, we had seen but two seals. We were transfixed by the young bear. We watched him move off across the ice, into a confusing plane of grays and whites. . . . A snow shower moved quickly through, and when it cleared we could barely make him out in the black water with field glasses from the rocking boat. A young and successful hunter, at home in his home.

He had found the seals.

BARRY LOPEZ, 1945–

CHARLES S. RALEIGH, *Law of the Wild*, 1881

First Relations

Part of the darkness lived. Furred or scaled
according to its mood, it crawled or bounded, snorted
or drooled, it swam or ripped bark from trees,
and it was powerful because it could do all these things at once
and because it could show itself or transmogrify
into boulder, log, hummock of grass. We gave it our fear
freely and bountifully so it would not take more of us;
we made words and gave it a name we never spoke.
Still it pressed so close we tasted its breath, felt our bones
seized. And so we slept with fire, which we also feared.
Children rose up, blood-hot, hungry. We were many.
Some of us predicted its shapes from clouds, some
studied its scents, some imitated its calls and silences;
and we followed it everywhere, darkness in our hands.

PAMELA ALEXANDER, 1948–

HENRI ROUSSEAU, *Tropical Forest with Monkeys*, 1910

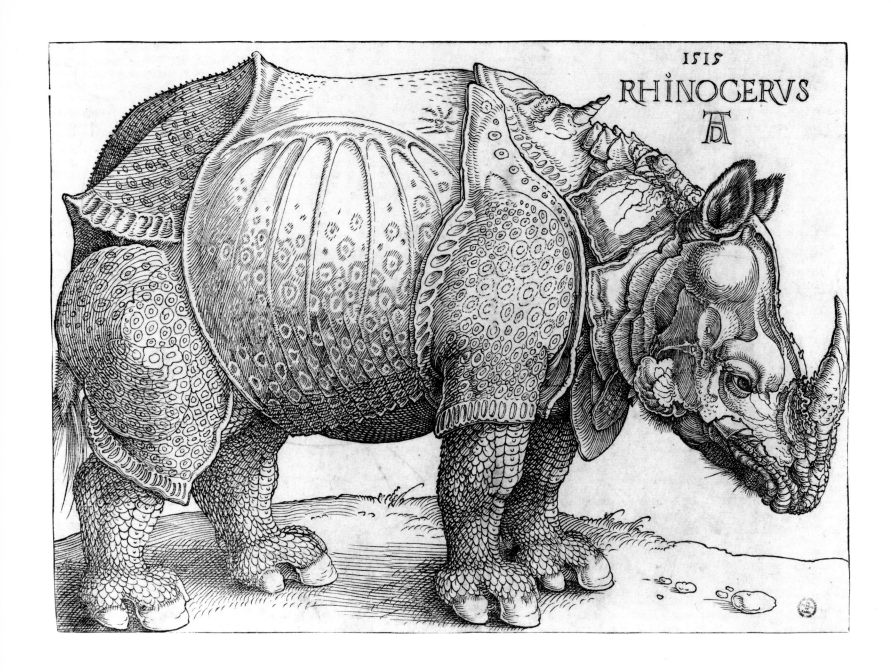

ALBRECHT DÜRER, *The Rhinoceros*, 1515

The Rhinoceros

The rhino is a homely beast,
For human eyes he's not a feast.
Farewell, farewell, you old rhinoceros,
I'll stare at something less prepoceros.

OGDEN NASH, 1902–1971

The Tyger

Tyger! Tyger! burning bright
In the forests of the night,
What immortal hand or eye
Could frame thy fearful symmetry?

In what distant deeps or skies
Burnt the fire of thine eyes?
On what wings dare he aspire?
What the hand, dare seize the fire?

And what shoulder, & what art,
Could twist the sinews of thy heart?
And when thy heart began to beat,
What dread hand? & what dread feet?

What the hammer? what the chain?
In what furnace was thy brain?
What the anvil? what dread grasp
Dare its deadly terrors clasp?

When the stars threw down their spears,
And water'd heaven with their tears,
Did he smile his work to see?
Did he who made the Lamb make thee?

Tyger! Tyger! burning bright
In the forests of the night,
What immortal hand or eye
Dare frame thy fearful symmetry?

WILLIAM BLAKE, 1757–1827

from Apology for Raimond Sebond

As for clemency, they tell of a tiger, the most inhuman of all beasts, that, having been given a kid, he endured hunger for two days before being willing to harm it; and the third day he broke the cage in which he was confined, to go in search of other food, being unwilling to attack the kid, his companion and guest.

MICHEL EYQUEM DE MONTAIGNE, 1533–1592

SIR PETER PAUL RUBENS,
Daniel in the Lions' Den, C. 1613/1615

IO

September Midnight

Lyric night of the lingering Indian Summer,
Shadowy fields that are scentless but full of singing,
Never a bird, but the passionless chant of insects,
      Ceaseless, insistent.

The grasshopper's horn, and far-off, high in the maples,
The wheel of a locust leisurely grinding the silence
Under a moon waning and worn, broken,
      Tired with summer.

Let me remember you, voices of little insects,
Weeds in the moonlight, fields that are tangled with asters,
Let me remember, soon will the winter be on us,
      Snow-hushed and heavy.

Over my soul murmur your mute benediction,
While I gaze, O fields that rest after harvest,
As those who part look long in the eyes they lean to,
      Lest they forget them.

SARA TEASDALE, 1884–1933 FROM *Love Songs*

JACOB LAWRENCE, *Daybreak — A Time to Rest*, 1967

Tyranny of Moths

tonight the moths
go stitching with their kind
up and down the net

they may never know
my light is not my day

they seem so harried
poor peasants in a war

their bodies
would disturb my reading light

my life tonight

switching out the light
we are drawn to another light
farther down the road

GERALD VIZENOR, 1934–

ARTHUR G. DOVE, *Moth Dance*, 1929

The Maldive Shark

About the Shark, phlegmatical one,
Pale sot of the Maldive sea,
The sleek little pilot-fish, azure and slim,
How alert in attendance be.
From his saw-pit of mouth, from his charnel of maw
They have nothing of harm to dread,
But liquidly glide on his ghastly flank
Or before his Gorgonian head;
Or lurk in the port of serrated teeth
In white triple tiers of glittering gates,
And there find a haven when peril's abroad,
An asylum in jaws of the Fates!

They are friends; and friendly they guide him to prey,
Yet never partake of the treat —
Eyes and brains to the dotard lethargic and dull,
Pale ravener of horrible meat.

HERMAN MELVILLE, 1819–1891

An Egyptian Pulled Glass Bottle in the Shape of a Fish

Here we have thirst
And patience, from the first,
      And art, as in a wave held up for us to see
      In its essential perpendicularity;

Not brittle but
Intense — the spectrum, that
      Spectacular and humble animal the fish,
      Whose scales turn aside the sun's sword with their polish.

MARIANNE MOORE, 1887–1972

DUCCIO DI BUONINSEGNA, *The Calling of the Apostles Peter and Andrew*, 1308/1311

Eulogy for a Hermit Crab

You were consistently brave
On these surf-drenched rocks, in and out of their salty
Slough holes around which the entire expanse
Of the glinting grey sea and the single spotlight
Of the sun went spinning and spinning and spinning
In a tangle of blinding spume and spray
And pistol-shot collisions your whole life long.
You stayed. Even with the wet icy wind of the moon
Circling your silver case night after night after night
You were here.

And by the gritty orange curve of your claws,
By the soft, wormlike grip
Of your hinter body, by the unrelieved wonder
Of your black-pea eyes, by the mystified swing
And swing and swing of your touching antennae,
You maintained your name meticulously, you kept
Your name intact exactly, day after day after day.
No one could say you were less than perfect
In the hermitage of your crabness.

Now, beside the racing, incomprehensible racket
Of the sea stretching its great girth forever
Back and forth between this direction and another,
Please let the words of this proper praise I speak
Become the identical and proper sound
Of my mourning.

PATTIANN ROGERS, 1940–

ITALIAN (PADUAN), *Box in the Form of a Crab,*
LATE 15TH OR EARLY 16TH CENTURY

The Frog

Be kind and tender to the Frog,
        And do not call him names,
As 'Slimy skin,' or 'Polly-wog,'
        Or likewise 'Ugly James,'
Or 'Gap-a-grin,' or 'Toad-gone-wrong,'
        Or 'Bill Bandy-knees':
The Frog is justly sensitive
        To epithets like these.
No animal will more repay
        A treatment kind and fair;
At least so lonely people say
Who keep a frog (and, by the way,
They are extremely rare).

HILAIRE BELLOC, 1870–1953
FROM *The Bad Child's Book of Beasts*

PADUAN, *A Frog*, EARLY 16TH CENTURY

Is It Morning? Is It the Little Morning?

Is it morning? Is it the little morning
Just before dawn? How big the sun is!
Are those the birds? Their voices begin
Everywhere, whistling, piercing, and joyous
All over and in the air, speaking the words
Which are more than words, with mounting consciousness:
And everything begins to rise to the brightening
Of the slow light that ascends to the blaze's lightning!

DELMORE SCHWARTZ, 1913–1966

WINSLOW HOMER, *Right and Left*, 1909

from Notes

Where go the birds when the rain
Roars and sweeps and fells the grain,
When tortured trees groan with pain,
And the storm-worn night is old —
Driven forth from their slumber cold,
Where go the birds?

JANE HEAP, EARLY TWENTIETH CENTURY

The eagle wants no friends

The eagle wants no friends,
employs his thoughts to other ends —
he has his circles to inscribe
twelve thousand feet from where
the fishes comb the sea,
he finds his solace in unscathed
immensity,
where eagles think, there is no need
of being lonesome —
In isolation
is a deep revealing sense
of home.

MARSDEN HARTLEY, 1877–1943

TITIAN, *Study of an Eagle*, C. 1515

The Bird

Adventurous bird walking upon the air,
Like a schoolboy running and loitering, leaping
   and springing,
Pensively pausing, suddenly changing your mind
To turn at ease on the heel of a wing-tip. Where
In all the crystalline world was there to find
For your so delicate walking and airy winging
A floor so perfect, so firm and so fair,
And where a ceiling and walls so sweetly ringing,
Whenever you sing, to your clear singing?

The wide-winged soul itself can ask no more
Than such a pure, resilient and endless floor
For its strong-pinioned plunging and soaring and
   upward and upward springing.

EDWIN MUIR, 1887–1959

ANDREA MANTEGNA, *Bird Perched on a Branch with Fruit*, C. 1495

Humming-Bird

I can imagine, in some otherworld
Primeval-dumb, far back
In that most awful stillness, that only gasped and hummed,
Humming-birds raced down the avenues.

Before anything had a soul,
While life was a heave of Matter, half inanimate,
This little bit chipped off in brilliance
And went whizzing through the slow, vast, succulent stems.

I believe there were no flowers then,
In the world where the humming-bird flashed ahead of creation.
I believe he pierced the slow vegetable veins with his long beak.

Probably he was big
As mosses, and little lizards, they say, were once big.
Probably he was a jabbing, terrifying monster.

We look at him through the wrong end of the telescope of Time,
Luckily for us.

D. H. LAWRENCE, 1885–1930

MARTIN JOHNSON HEADE, *Cattleya Orchid and Three Brazilian Hummingbirds*, 1871

Thrise happie hee, who by some shadie Grove

Thrise happie hee, who by some shadie Grove
Farre from the clamorous World doth live his owne,
Though solitarie, yet who is not alone,
But doth converse with that *Eternall Love*.
O how more sweet is Birds harmonious Mone,
Or the soft Sobbings of the widow'd Dove?
Than those smoothe Whisp'rings neare a Princes Throne,
Which Good make doubtfull, doe the Evill approve.
O how more sweet is *Zephyres* wholesome Breath,
And Sighs perfum'd, which doe the Flowres unfold,
Than that Applause vaine *Honour* doth bequeath?
How sweete are Streames to Poyson drunke in Golde?
    The World is full of Horrours, Falshoods, Slights,
    Woods silent Shades have only true Delights.

WILLIAM DRUMMOND, 1585–1649

FRANÇOIS BOUCHER, *Venus Consoling Love*, 1751

Well now, the virgin . . .

Well now, the virgin and the unicorn —
Although its point and details are obscure
The theme speeds up the pulses, to be sure.
No doubt it is the thought of that long horn
Inclined towards a lady young, well-born,
Unfearful, naïve, soft, ecstatic, pure.
How often, dreaming, have we found the cure
For our malaise, to tear or to be torn!

In fact, the beast and virgin merely sat,
I seem to think, in some enameled field;
He milky, muscular, and she complete
In kirtle, bodice, wimple. Even that
Tame conjugation makes our eyeballs yield
Those gems we long to cast at someone's feet.

ROY FULLER, 1912–1991

BERNARDINO LUINI, *Procris and the Unicorn*, C. 1520/1522

Whoso list to hunt . . .

Whoso list to hunt, I know where is an hind,
    But as for me — alas, I may no more.
    The vain travail hath wearied me so sore,
    I am of them that farthest cometh behind.
Yet may I, by no means, my wearied mind
    Draw from the deer; but as she fleeth afore
    Fainting I follow. I leave off therefore,
    Since in a net I seek to hold the wind.
Who list her hunt, I put him out of doubt,
    As well as I, may spend his time in vain.
    And graven with diamonds in letters plain
There is written, her fair neck round about:
    Noli me tangere, for Caesar's I am,
    And wild for to hold, though I seem tame.

SIR THOMAS WYATT, 1503–1542

ALBRECHT DÜRER, *St. Eustace*, C. 1500/1501

Circe

The Palace in a woody vale they found,
High rais'd of stone; a shaded space around:
Where mountain wolves and brindled lions roam,
(By magic tam'd) familiar to the dome.
With gentle blandishment our men they meet,
And wag their tails, and fawning lick their feet.
As from some feast a man returning late,
His faithful dogs all meet him at the gate,
Rejoycing round, some morsel to receive,
(Such as the good man ever us'd to give.)
Domestick thus the griesly beasts drew near;
They gaze with wonder, not unmixt with fear.
Now on the threshold of the dome they stood,
And heard a voice resounding thro' the wood:
Plac'd at her loom within, the Goddess sung;
The vaulted roofs and solid pavement rung. . . .

What voice celestial, chaunting to the loom
(Or Nymph, or Goddess) ecchos from the room?
Say shall we seek access? With that they call;
And wide unfold the portals of the hall.

The Goddess rising, asks her guests to stay,
Who blindly follow where she leads the way.
Eurylochus alone of all the band,
Suspecting fraud, more prudently remain'd.

On thrones around, with downy coverings grac'd,
With semblance fair th' unhappy men she plac'd.
Milk newly prest, the sacred flow'r of wheat,
And honey fresh, and *Pramnian* wines the treat:
But venom'd was the bread, and mix'd the bowl,
With drugs of force to darken all the soul:
Soon in the luscious feast themselves they lost,
And drank oblivion of their native coast.
Instant her circling wand the Goddess waves,
To hogs transforms 'em, and the Sty receives.
No more was seen the human form divine,
Head, face and members bristle into swine:
Still curst with sense, their mind remains alone,
And their own voice affrights them when they groan.
Mean-while the Goddess in disdain bestows
The mast and acorn, brutal food! and strows
The fruits of cornel, as their feast, around;
Now prone, and groveling on unsav'ry ground.

HOMER, NINTH CENTURY B.C. FROM *The Odyssey*
translated by
ALEXANDER POPE, 1688–1744

DOSSO DOSSI, *Circe and Her Lovers in a Landscape*, C. 1525

Small Animal

have I found you?
Your den is narrow, has many holes,
but earth is hollow under the spruce log
and bare by the white stone,
and grass is broken on the bank.

Snow has lain two days now, and no tracks.
You're warm or asleep or afraid.

Yet I'm no trap.
If I knew your food, I'd bring it.
I'd kill for you
whom I've never seen.

I'd put my arm deep into your den,
who are my only chance
for a wet nose in the hand
or teeth.

ALBERTA TURNER, 1919–

HANS HOFFMANN, *Red Squirrel,* 1578

from Walden

The hares . . . were very familiar. One had her form under my house all winter, separated from me only by the flooring, and she startled me each morning by her hasty departure when I began to stir, — thump, thump, thump, striking her head against the floor timbers in her hurry. They used to come round my door at dusk to nibble the potato parings which I had thrown out, and were so nearly the color of the ground that they could hardly be distinguished when still. Sometimes in the twilight I alternately lost and recovered sight of one sitting motionless under my window. When I opened my door in the evening, off they would go with a squeak and a bounce. Near at hand they only excited my pity. One evening one sat by my door two paces from me, at first trembling with fear, yet unwilling to move; a poor wee thing, lean and bony, with ragged ears and sharp nose, scant tail and slender paws. It looked as if Nature no longer contained the breed of nobler bloods, but stood on her last toes. Its large eyes appeared young and unhealthy, almost dropsical. I took a step, and lo, away it scud with an elastic spring over the snow crust, straightening its body and its limbs into graceful length, and soon put the forest between me and itself, — the wild free venison, asserting its vigor and the dignity of Nature. Not without reason was its slenderness.

HENRY DAVID THOREAU, 1817–1862

JOHN JAMES AUDUBON, *Arctic Hare*, C. 1841

The Thought-Fox

I imagine this midnight moment's forest:
Something else is alive
Beside the clock's loneliness
And this blank page where my fingers move.

Through the window I see no star:
Something more near
Though deeper within darkness
Is entering the loneliness:

Cold, delicately as the dark snow
A fox's nose touches twig, leaf;
Two eyes serve a movement, that now
And again now, and now, and now

Sets neat prints into the snow
Between trees, and warily a lame
Shadow lags by stump and in hollow
Of a body that is bold to come

Across clearings, and eye,
A widening deepening greenness,
Brilliantly, concentratedly,
Coming about its own business

Till, with a sudden sharp hot stink of fox
It enters the dark hole of the head.
The window is starless still; the clock ticks,
The page is printed.

TED HUGHES, 1930–

AGNES MILLER PARKER, *Fox*, 1940

Fox   99/250.   1940

D. G. Stouter

Sacrament

God, I have sought you as a fox seeks chickens,
curbing my hunger with cunning.
The times I have tasted your flesh
there was no bread and wine between us,
only night and the wind beating the grass.

ALDEN NOWLAN, 1933–1983

from Pastoralls, The Fourth Eglogue

When first religion with a golden chayne,
Men unto fayre civilitie did draw,
Who sent from heaven, brought justice forth againe,
To keepe the good, the viler·sort to awe. . . .
The tender grasse was then the softest bed:
The pleasant'st shades esteem'd the statelyest halls,
No belly-churle with Bacchus banqueted,
Nor painted rags then covered rotten walls: . . .
But when the bowels of the earth were sought,
Whose golden entrailes mortalls did espie,
Into the world all mischiefe then was brought,
This fram'd the mint, that coyn'd our miserie.
The loftie pines were presently hew'd downe,
And men, sea-monsters swam the bracky flood,
In wainscote tubs to seeke out worlds unknowne,
For certayne ill, to leave assured good.
The steed was tamde and fitted to the field,
That serves a subject to the riders lawes,
He that before ranne in the pastures wyld,
Felt the stiffe curbe controule his angrie jaws.

The Cyclops then stood sweating to the fire,
The use thereof in softning metals found,
That did streight limbs in stubborne steele attire,
Forging sharpe tooles the tender flesh to wound.
The citie-builder, then intrencht his towres,
And laid his wealth within the walled towne,
Which afterward in rough and stormie stowres,
Kindled the fire that burnt his bulwarkes downe.
This was the sad beginning of our woe,
That was from hell on wretched mortals hurl'd,
And from this fount did all those mischiefes flow,
Whose inundation drowneth all the world.

MICHAEL DRAYTON, 1563–1631

JOSEPH ANDERSON FARIS, *The Neigh of an Iron Horse*, 1860s

The Flower-fed Buffaloes

The flower-fed buffaloes of the spring
In the days of long ago,
Ranged where the locomotives sing
And the prairie flowers lie low:
The tossing, blooming, perfumed grass
Is swept away by the wheat,
Wheels and wheels and wheels spin by
In the spring that still is sweet.
But the flower-fed buffaloes of the spring
Left us, long ago.
They gore no more, they bellow no more,
They trundle around the hills no more:
With the Blackfeet, lying low.
With the Pawnees, lying low,
Lying low.

VACHEL LINDSAY, 1879–1931

JOHN MARIN, *Sketch of Two Bison*, C. 1950

I Ride an Old Paint

I ride an old Paint and I lead an old Dan,
I'm going to Montan' for to throw the hoolihan,
They feed in the coolees, they water in the draw,
Tails are all matted, their backs are all raw.
    Ride around, little dogies, ride around them slow,
    The fiery and the snuffy are raring to go.

I've worked in the town and I've worked on the farm,
And all I got to show is just this muscle in my arm;
Got a blister on my foot, got a callus on my hand,
But I'll be a cowpuncher long as I can.
    Ride around, little dogies, ride around them slow,
    The fiery and the snuffy are raring to go. . . .

When I die, take my saddle from the wall
And lead my old pony out of his stall;
Tie my bones to his saddle, turn our faces toward the west,
We'll ride the prairies that we love the best.
    Ride around, little dogies, ride around them slow,
    The fiery and the snuffy are raring to go.

COWBOY SONG

AMERICAN, *Spring on the Range*, LAST QUARTER 19TH CENTURY

from Prothalamion

With that I saw two Swannes of goodly hewe,
Come softly swimming downe along the Lee;
Two fairer Birds I yet did never see:
The snow which doth the top of *Pindus* strew,
Did never whiter shew,
Nor *Jove* himselfe when he a Swan would be
For love of *Leda,* whiter did appeare:
Yet *Leda* was they say as white as he,
Yet not so white as these, nor nothing neare;
So purely white they were,
That even the gentle streame, the which them bare,
Seem'd foule to them, and bad his billowes spare
To wet their silken feathers, least they might
Soyle their fayre plumes with water not so fayre,
And marre their beauties bright,
That shone as heavens light,
Against their Brydale day, which was not long:
 Sweete *Themmes* runne softly, till I end my Song.

EDMUND SPENSER, C. 1552–1599

JOHN CONSTABLE,
Wivenhoe Park, Essex, 1816

54

H. CALL, *Prize Bull*, 1876

Pied Beauty

Glory be to God for dappled things —
> For skies of couple-colour as a brinded cow;
>> For rose-moles all in stipple upon trout that swim;
Fresh-firecoal chestnut-falls; finches' wings;
> Landscape plotted and pieced — fold, fallow, and plough;
>> And áll trádes, their gear and tackle and trim.
All things counter, original, spare, strange;
> Whatever is fickle, freckled (who knows how?)
>> With swift, slow; sweet, sour; adazzle, dim;
He fathers-forth whose beauty is past change:
>>>> Praise him.

GERARD MANLEY HOPKINS, 1844–1889

from The White Peacock

Though there was plenty of room for ten yet they shouldered and shoved and struggled to capture a larger space, and many little trotters dabbled and spilled the stuff, and the ten sucking, clapping snouts twitched fiercely, and twenty little eyes glared askance, like so many points of wrath.

They gave uneasy, gasping grunts in their haste. The unhappy eleventh rushed from point to point trying to push in his snout, but for his pains he got rough squeezing, and sharp grabs on his ears. Then he lifted up his face and screamed screams of grief and wrath unto the evening sky. But the ten little gluttons only twitched their ears to make sure there was no danger in the noise and then sucked harder with much spilling and slobbing. George laughed like a sardonic Jove, but at last gave ear, and kicked the ten little gluttons from the trough and allowed the residue to the eleventh. This one, poor wretch almost wept with relief as he sucked and swallowed in sobs, casting his little eyes apprehensively upwards although he did not lift his nose from the trough, as he heard the vindictive shrieks of the ten little fiends kept at bay by George. The solitary feeder, shivering with apprehension, rubbed the wood bare with his snout, and then turning up to the heaven his eyes of gratitude reluctantly left the trough.

D. H. LAWRENCE, 1885–1930

ALBRECHT DÜRER,
The Prodigal Son, C. 1496

MARTIN SCHONGAUER,
Family of Pigs, C. 1480/1490

Cock-Crow

Out of the wood of thoughts that grows by night
To be cut down by the sharp axe of light, —
Out of the night, two cocks together crow,
Cleaving the darkness with a silver blow:
And bright before my eyes twin trumpeters stand,
Heralds of splendour, one at either hand,
Each facing each as in a coat of arms:
The milkers lace their boots up at the farms.

EDWARD THOMAS, 1878–1917

Bantams in Pine-Woods

Chieftain Iffucan of Azcan in caftan
Of tan with henna hackles, halt!

Damned universal cock, as if the sun
Was blackamoor to bear your blazing tail.

Fat! Fat! Fat! Fat! I am the personal.
Your world is you. I am my world.

You ten-foot poet among inchlings. Fat!
Begone! An inchling bristles in these pines,

Bristles, and points their Appalachian tangs,
And fears not portly Azcan nor his hoos.

WALLACE STEVENS, 1879–1955

NIGERIAN, COURT OF BENIN, *Fowl*, PROBABLY MID-18TH CENTURY

An Indian summer view of the Farm & stock of JAMES C. CORNELL of Northampton Bucks county Pennsylvania. That took the Premium

from Birds and Poets

[The cow] has not the classic beauty of the horse, but in picture-making qualities she is far ahead of him. Her shaggy, loose-jointed body; her irregular, sketchy outlines, like those of the landscape, — the hollows and ridges, the slopes and prominences; her tossing horns, her bushy tail, her swinging gait, her tranquil, ruminating habits, — all tend to make her an object upon which the artist eye loves to dwell. The artists are forever putting her into pictures, too. In rural landscape scenes she is an important feature. Behold her grazing in the pastures and on the hillsides, or along banks of streams, or ruminating under wide-spreading trees, or standing belly-deep in the creek or pond, or lying upon the smooth places in the quiet summer afternoon, the day's grazing done, and waiting to be summoned home to be milked; and again in the twilight lying upon the level summit of the hill, or where the sward is thickest and softest; or in winter a herd of them filing along toward the spring to drink, or being "foddered" from the stack in the field upon the new snow, — surely the cow is a picturesque animal, and all her goings and comings are pleasant to behold.

JOHN BURROUGHS, 1837–1921

EDWARD HICKS, *The Cornell Farm*, 1848

Coming to the Salt Lick

They will have it.
But not in the fodder
blowing ropily green
from their yellow mouths.

Now they are coming down from the pasture,
the swinging bell, the milky blaze,
heavy, imprecise, to the acrid stone.

Why do they want it?
Why do we need it?

It is our blood, remembering its own taste,
and when we took different paths
in the forest.

JOHN WOODS, 1926–

PAUL GAUGUIN, *Haystacks in Brittany,* 1890

The Oven Bird

There is a singer everyone has heard,
Loud, a midsummer and a mid-wood bird,
Who makes the solid tree trunks sound again.
He says that leaves are old and that for flowers
Midsummer is to spring as one to ten.
He says the early petal-fall is past
When pear and cherry bloom went down in showers
On sunny days a moment overcast;
And comes that other fall we name the fall.
He says the highway dust is over all.
The bird would cease and be as other birds
But that he knows in singing not to sing.
The question that he frames in all but words
Is what to make of a diminished thing.

ROBERT FROST, 1874–1963

CHARLES V. BOND, *Still Life: Fruit, Bird, and Dwarf Pear Tree*, 1856

Job 39:19–25

Hast thou given the horse strength? hast thou clothed his neck with thunder?

Canst thou make him afraid as a grasshopper? the glory of his nostrils is terrible.

He paweth in the valley, and rejoiceth in his strength: he goeth on to meet the armed men.

He mocketh at fear, and is not affrighted; neither turneth he back from the sword.

The quiver rattleth against him, the glittering spear and the shield.

He swalloweth the ground with fierceness and rage: neither believeth he that it is the sound of the trumpet.

He saith among the trumpets, Ha, ha; and he smelleth the battle afar off, the thunder of the captains, and the shouting.

FROM *The King James Bible*

ALBRECHT DÜRER, *Knight, Death and Devil*, 1513

When I Went to the Circus

When I went to the circus that had pitched on the waste lot
it was full of uneasy people
frightened of the bare earth and the temporary canvas
and the smell of horses and other beasts
instead of merely the smell of man.

Monkeys rode rather grey and wizened
on curly plump piebald ponies
and the children uttered a little cry —
and dogs jumped through hoops and turned somersaults
and then the geese scuttled in in a little flock
and round the ring they went to the sound of the whip
then doubled, and back, with a funny up-flutter of wings —
and the children suddenly shouted out.

Then came the hush again, like a hush of fear.

The tight-rope lady, pink and blonde and nude-looking,
    with a few gold spangles
footed cautiously out on the rope, turned prettily, spun round
bowed, and lifted her foot in her hand, smiled, swung her parasol
to another balance, tripped round, poised, and slowly sank
her handsome thighs down, down, till she slept her splendid body
    on the rope.
When she rose, tilting her parasol, and smiled at the cautious people
they cheered, but nervously.

The trapeze man, slim and beautiful and like a fish in the air
swung great curves through the upper space, and came down
    like a star
— And the people applauded, with hollow, frightened applause.

The elephants, huge and grey, loomed their curved bulk
    through the dusk
and sat up, taking strange postures, showing the pink soles
    of their feet
and curling their precious live trunks like ammonites
and moving always with a soft slow precision
as when a great ship moves to anchor.
The people watched and wondered, and seemed to resent the
    mystery that lies in beasts.

JOHN STEUART CURRY, *Circus Elephants*, 1932

W. H. BROWN, *Bareback Riders*, 1886

Horses, gay horses, swirling round and plaiting
in a long line, their heads laid over each other's necks;
they were happy, they enjoyed it;
all the creatures seemed to enjoy the game
in the circus, with their circus people.

But the audience, compelled to wonder
compelled to admire the bright rhythms of moving bodies
compelled to see the delicate skill of flickering human bodies
flesh flamey and a little heroic, even in a tumbling clown,
they were not really happy.
There was no gushing response, as there is at the film.

When modern people see the carnal body dauntless and
    flickering gay
playing among the elements neatly, beyond competition
and displaying no personality,
modern people are depressed.

Modern people feel themselves at a disadvantage.
They know they have no bodies that could play among
    the elements.
They have only their personalities, that are best seen flat,
    on the film,
flat personalities in two dimensions,
    imponderable and touchless.

And they grudge the circus people the swooping gay weight
    of limbs
that flower in mere movement,
and they grudge them the immediate, physical understanding
    they have with their circus beasts,
and they grudge them their circus-life altogether.

Yet the strange, almost frightened shout of delight that comes
    now and then from the children
shows that the children vaguely know how cheated they are of
    their birthright
in the bright wild circus flesh.

D. H. LAWRENCE, 1885–1930

Pot-Luck among the Casuals

A dog came loping to his side
have you any of a speechless bone
no — but I have foul weathers in
my head,
and why should you want another one
you who are all but wrack of bone
and nearly dead,
why — very wind plays tunes upon
your ribs — the birds could build a nest
in the hollow of your spine
who is it fed you on broken stone
you walking, pallid skeleton?

he gave him a hunk of what he had
'tis good enough for me — none, or so he said,
when you want to go, is sweeter —
from worse to something better;
bone will maybe sharpen teeth
but makes pain sharper underneath —
a bowl of downright summer blood
would do you heaps of good.

the dog looked up to him and said,
save me — save me from a speedy grave
give anything of what you have;
he gave two hunks of what he little had
it was as if his jaw would crack
it felt so good —
a smile came out of canine face
and fairly shamed the listless place —
a dog that wants, is tragical to see —
we're used to men that get that way.

MARSDEN HARTLEY, 1877–1943

PIERRE BONNARD, *Two Dogs in a Deserted Street*, C. 1894

The Snakes of September

All summer I heard them
rustling in the shrubbery,
outracing me from tier
to tier in my garden,
a whisper among the viburnums,
a signal flashed from the hedgerow,
a shadow pulsing
in the barberry thicket.
Now that the nights are chill
and the annuals spent,
I should have thought them gone,
in a torpor of blood
slipped to the nether world
before the sickle frost.
Not so. In the deceptive balm
of noon, as if defiant of the curse
that spoiled another garden,
these two appear on show
through a narrow slit
in the dense green brocade
of a north-country spruce,
dangling head-down, entwined
in a brazen love-knot.
I put out my hand and stroke
the fine, dry grit of their skins.

After all,
we are partners in this land,
co-signers of a covenant.
At my touch the wild
braid of creation
trembles.

STANLEY KUNITZ, 1905–

PAUL GAUGUIN, *Self-Portrait*, 1889

from The Wants of Man

I want a warm and faithful friend,
    To cheer the adverse hour,
Who ne'er to flatter will descend,
    Nor bend the knee to power;
A friend to chide me when I'm wrong,
    My inmost soul to see;
And that my friendship prove as strong
    For him, as his for me.

JOHN QUINCY ADAMS, 1767–1848

AMERICAN, *The Dog*, EARLY 20TH CENTURY

from The Task

Drawn from his refuge in some lonely elm

That age or injury has hollow'd deep,

Where, on his bed of wool and matted leaves

He has outslept the winter, ventures forth

To frisk awhile, and bask in the warm sun,

The squirrel, flippant, pert, and full of play:

He sees me, and at once, swift as a bird

Ascends the neighbouring beech; there whisks his brush,

And perks his ears, and stamps, and cries aloud

With all the prettiness of feign'd alarm

And anger insignificantly fierce.

WILLIAM COWPER, 1731–1800

THE DENISON LIMNER, *Miss Denison of Stonington, Connecticut (possibly Matilda Denison)*, C. 1790

Hen's Nest

Among the orchard weeds, from every search,
Snugly and sure, the old hen's nest is made,
Who cackles every morning from her perch
To tell the servant girl new eggs are laid;
Who lays her washing by; and far and near
Goes seeking all about from day to day,
And stung with nettles tramples everywhere;
But still the cackling pullet lays away.
The boy on Sundays goes the stack to pull
In hopes to find her there, but naught is seen,
And takes his hat and thinks to find it full,
She's laid so long so many might have been.
But naught is found and all is given o'er
Till the young brood come chirping to the door.

JOHN CLARE, 1793–1864

AUGUSTE RENOIR, *Madame Monet and Her Son*, 1874

from Phylyp Sparowe

That vengeaunce I aske and crye,
By way of exclamacyon,
Of all the whole nacyon
Of cattes wylde and tame;
God send them sorowe and shame!
That cat especyally
That slew so cruelly
My lytell pretty sparowe,
That I brought up at Carowe.
O cat of churlyshe kynde,
The Fynde was in thy minde
When thou my byrde untwynde!
I would thou haddest ben blynde!
The leopardes savage,
The lyons in theyr rage,
Myght catche thee in theyr pawes!
And gnawe thee in theyr jawes!
The serpentes of Lybany
Myght stynge thee venymously!
The dragones with theyr tonges
Myght poyson thy lyver and longes!
The mantycors of the montaynes
Myght fede them on thy braynes!
Melanchates, that hounde
That plucked Actæon to the grounde,
Gave hym his mortall wounde,
Chaunged to a dere,

The story doth appere,
Was chaunged to an harte:
So thou, foule cat that thou arte,
The selfesame hounde
Myght thee confounde,
That his owne lord bote,
Myght byte asondre thy throte!
Of Inde the gredy grypes
Myght tere out all thy trypes!
Of Arcady the beares
Myght plucke awaye thyne eares!
The wylde wolfe Lycaon
Byte asondre thy backe bone!
Of Ethna the brennynge hyll,
That day and nyghte brenneth styl,
Set in thy tayle a blase,
That all the world may gase
And wonder upon thee!
From Ocyan the greate sea
Unto the Isles of Orchady;
From Tyllbery ferry
To the playne of Salysbery!
So trayterously my byrde to kyll,
That never wrought thee evyll wyll!

JOHN SKELTON, C. 1460–1529

AMERICAN, *The Cat*, PROBABLY 1850/1899

from Jubilate Agno

For I will consider my Cat Jeoffrey.

For he is the servant of the Living God, duly and daily serving him.

For at the First glance of the glory of God in the East he worships in his way.

For is this done by wreathing his body seven times round with elegant quickness.

For then he leaps up to catch the musk, which is the blessing of God upon his prayer.

For he rolls upon prank to work it in.

For having done duty and received blessing he begins to consider himself.

For this he performs in ten degrees.

For first he looks upon his fore-paws to see if they are clean.

For secondly he kicks up behind to clear away there.

For thirdly he works it upon stretch with the fore-paws extended.

For fourthly he sharpens his paws by wood.

For fifthly he washes himself.

For sixthly he rolls upon wash.

For Seventhly he fleas himself, that he may not be interrupted upon the beat.

For Eighthly he rubs himself against a post.

For Ninthly he looks up for his instructions.

For Tenthly he goes in quest of food.

For having consider'd God and himself he will consider his neighbour.

For if he meets another cat he will kiss her in kindness.

For when he takes his prey he plays with it to give it a chance.

For one mouse in seven escapes by his dallying.

For when his day's work is done his business more properly begins.

For he keeps the Lord's watch in the night against the adversary.

CHRISTOPHER SMART, 1722–1771

AUGUSTE RENOIR, *Woman with a Cat*, C. 1875

from The White and Black Dynasties

To gain the friendship of a cat is not an easy thing. It is a philosophic, well-regulated, tranquil animal, a creature of habit and a lover of order and cleanliness. It does not give its affections indiscriminately. It will consent to be your friend if you are worthy of the honour, but it will not be your slave. With all its affection, it preserves its freedom of judgment, and it will not do anything for you which it considers unreasonable; but once it has given its love, what absolute confidence, what fidelity of affection! It will make itself the companion of your hours of work, of loneliness, or of sadness. It will lie the whole evening on your knee, purring and happy in your society, and leaving the company of creatures of its own kind to be with you. In vain the sound of caterwauling reverberates from the house-tops, inviting it to one of those cats' evening parties where essence of red-herring takes the place of tea. It will not be tempted, but continues to keep its vigil with you. If you put it down it climbs up again quickly, with a sort of crooning noise, which is like a gentle reproach. Sometimes, when seated in front of you, it gazes at you with such soft, melting eyes, such a human and caressing look, that you are almost awed, for it seems impossible that reason can be absent from it.

THÉOPHILE GAUTIER, 1811–1872

EDOUARD VUILLARD, *Théodore Duret*, 1912

Two Songs of a Fool

1

A speckled cat and a tame hare
Eat at my hearthstone
And sleep there;
And both look up to me alone
For learning and defence
As I look up to Providence.

I start out of my sleep to think
Some day I may forget
Their food and drink;
Or, the house door left unshut,
The hare may run till it's found
The horn's sweet note and the tooth of the hound.

I bear a burden that might well try
Men that do all by rule,
And what can I
That am a wandering-witted fool
But pray to God that He ease
My great responsibilities?

2

I slept on my three-legged stool by the fire,
The speckled cat slept on my knee;
We never thought to enquire
Where the brown hare might be,
And whether the door were shut.
Who knows how she drank the wind
Stretched up on two legs from the mat,
Before she had settled her mind
To drum with her heel and to leap?
Had I but awakened from sleep
And called her name, she had heard,
It may be, and had not stirred,
That now, it may be, has found
The horn's sweet note and the tooth of the hound.

WILLIAM BUTLER YEATS, 1865–1939

STURTEVANT J. HAMBLIN, *Little Girl with Pet Rabbit*, c. 1845

from A Letter to William Mason, May 22, 1781

You will find I have gotten a new idol, in a word, a successor to Rosette and almost as great a favourite, nor is this a breach of vows and constancy, but an act of piety. In a word, my poor dear old friend Madame du Deffand had a little dog of which she was extremely fond, and the last time I saw her she made me promise if I should survive her to take charge of it. I did. It is arrived and I was going to say, it is incredible how fond I am of it, but I have no occasion to brag of my dogmanity. I dined at Richmond House t'other day, and mentioning whither I was going, the Duke said, "Own the truth, shall not you call at home first and see Tonton?" He guessed rightly. He is now sitting on my paper as I write — not the Duke, but Tonton.

HORACE WALPOLE, 1717–1797

EDOUARD MANET, *A King Charles Spaniel*, C. 1866   MARY CASSATT, *Little Girl in a Blue Armchair*, 1878   93

Ulysses and His Dog

Thus, near the gates conferring as they drew,
Argus, the Dog, his ancient master knew;
He, not unconscious of the voice, and tread,
Lifts to the sound his ear, and rears his head.
Bred by *Ulysses,* nourish'd at his board,
But ah! not fated long to please his Lord!
To him, his swiftness and his strength were vain;
The voice of Glory call'd him o'er the main.
'Till then in ev'ry sylvan chace renown'd,
With *'Argus, Argus',* rung the woods around;
With him the youth pursu'd the goat or fawn,
Or trac'd the mazy leveret o'er the lawn.
Now left to man's ingratitude he lay,
Un-hous'd, neglected, in the publick way;
And where on heaps the rich manure was spread,
Obscene with reptile, took his sordid bed.

    He knew his Lord; he knew, and strove to meet,
In vain he strove, to crawl, and kiss his feet;
Yet (all he could) his tail, his ears, his eyes
Salute his master, and confess his joys.
Soft pity touch'd the mighty master's soul;
Adown his cheek a tear unbidden stole,
Stole unperceiv'd; he turn'd his head, and dry'd
The drop humane: then thus impassion'd cry'd.

    'What noble beast in this abandon'd state
Lies here all helpless at *Ulysses'* gate?
His bulk and beauty speak no vulgar praise;
If, as he seems, he was, in better days,
Some care his Age deserves: Or was he priz'd
For worthless beauty? therefore now despis'd?
Such dogs, and men there are, meer things of state,
And always cherish'd by their friends, the Great.'

    'Not *Argus* so' (*Eumaeus* thus rejoin'd)
'But serv'd a master of a nobler kind,
Who never, never shall behold him more!
Long, long since perish'd on a distant shore!
Oh had you seen him, vig'rous, bold and young,
Swift as a stag, and as a lion strong,
Him no fell Savage on the plain withstood,
None 'scap'd him, bosom'd in the gloomy wood;
His eye how piercing, and his scent how true,
To winde the vapour in the tainted dew?
Such, when *Ulysses* left his natal coast;
Now years un-nerve him, and his lord is lost!
The women keep the gen'rous creature bare,
A sleek and idle race is all their care.
The master gone, the servants what restrains?
Or dwells humanity where riot reigns?
Jove fix'd it certain, that whatever day
Makes man a slave, takes half his worth away.'

    This said, the honest herdsman strode before:
The musing Monarch pauses at the door:
The Dog whom Fate had granted to behold
His Lord, when twenty tedious years had roll'd,
Takes a last look, and having seen him, dies;
So clos'd for ever faithful *Argus'* eyes!

HOMER, NINTH CENTURY B.C., FROM *The Odyssey*
translated by ALEXANDER POPE, 1688–1744

EDWARD HOPPER, *Cape Cod Evening*, 1939

96

The Peace of Wild Things

When despair for the world grows in me
and I wake in the night at the least sound
in fear of what my life and my children's lives may be,
I go and lie down where the wood drake
rests in his beauty on the water, and the great heron feeds.
I come into the peace of wild things
who do not tax their lives with forethought
of grief. I come into the presence of still water.
And I feel above me the day-blind stars
waiting with their light. For a time
I rest in the grace of the world, and am free.

WENDELL BERRY, 1934–

98   EDWARD HICKS, *Peaceable Kingdom*, C. 1834

List of Works of Art

All works of art reproduced in this book are in the collections of the National Gallery of Art, Washington, D.C.

ENDPAPERS
Circle of Jan van Kessel, Flemish, 1626–1679
Study of Birds and Monkeys, 1660/1670
Oil on copper, 4$\frac{1}{16}$ x 6$\frac{3}{4}$ in. (10.4 x 17.2 cm)
Gift of John Dimick
1983.19.2

BAS-TITLE
Edward Hicks, American, 1780–1849
Peaceable Kingdom (detail), c. 1834
Oil on canvas, 30 x 35$\frac{1}{2}$ in. (76.2 x 90.2 cm)
Gift of Edgar William and Bernice Chrysler Garbisch
1980.62.15.(PA)

FRONTISPIECE
Sir Peter Paul Rubens, Flemish, 1577–1640
Lion, c. 1614
Black and yellow chalk heightened with white,
    9$\frac{15}{16}$ x 11$\frac{1}{8}$ in. (25.2 x 28.3 cm)
Ailsa Mellon Bruce Fund
1969.7.1.(DR)

PAGES VIII–1
Attributed to Jan van Kessel
Concert of Birds, 1660/1670
Oil on copper, 5$\frac{1}{8}$ x 7$\frac{1}{16}$ in. (13 x 8 cm)
Gift of John Dimick
1983.19.4

PAGE 3
Charles S. Raleigh, American, 1831–1925
Law of the Wild, 1881
Oil on canvas, 35$\frac{1}{8}$ x 40 in. (89.2 x 101.5 cm)
Gift of Edgar William and Bernice Chrysler Garbisch
1971.83.10

PAGES 4–5
Henri Rousseau, French, 1844–1910
Tropical Forest with Monkeys, 1910
Oil on linen, 51 x 64 in. (129.5 x 162.6 cm)
John Hay Whitney Collection
1982.76.7.(PA)

PAGE 6
Albrecht Dürer, German, 1471–1528
The Rhinoceros, 1515
Woodcut, 9$\frac{1}{4}$ x 11$\frac{3}{4}$ in. (23.5 x 29.8 cm)
Rosenwald Collection
1964.8.697.(PR)

PAGE 9
Eugène Delacroix, French, 1798–1863
Tiger, c. 1830
Watercolor, 5$\frac{9}{16}$ x 9$\frac{15}{16}$ in. (14.1 x 25.1 cm)
Rosenwald Collection
1943.3.3375.(DR)

PAGES 10–11
Sir Peter Paul Rubens
Daniel in the Lions' Den, c. 1613/1615
Canvas/oil on linen, 88$\frac{1}{4}$ x 130$\frac{1}{8}$ in. (224.3 x 330.4 cm)
Ailsa Mellon Bruce Fund
1965.13.1.(PA)

PAGE 13
Jacob Lawrence, American, 1917–
Daybreak — A Time to Rest, 1967
Tempera on hardboard, 30 x 24 in. (76.2 x 61 cm)
Anonymous gift
1973.8.1.(PA)

PAGE 15
Arthur G. Dove, American, 1880–1946
Moth Dance, 1929
Oil on canvas, 20 x 26$\frac{1}{8}$ in. (50.8 x 66.4 cm)
Alfred Stieglitz Collection
1949.2.1

PAGES 16–17
John Singleton Copley, American, 1738–1815
Watson and the Shark, 1778
Oil on canvas, 71$\frac{3}{4}$ x 90$\frac{1}{2}$ in. (182.1 x 229.7 cm)
Ferdinand Lammot Belin Fund
1963.6.1.(PA)

PAGE 19
Duccio di Buoninsegna, Sienese, c. 1255–1318
The Calling of the Apostles Peter and Andrew, 1308/1311
Tempera on panel, 17$\frac{1}{8}$ x 18$\frac{1}{8}$ in. (43.5 x 46 cm)
Samuel H. Kress Collection
1939.1.141.(PA)

PAGE 20
Italian (Paduan), 15th or 16th century
Box in the Form of a Crab, late 15th or early 16th century
Bronze sculpture, 1$\frac{7}{8}$ x 6$\frac{23}{32}$ x 3$\frac{21}{32}$ in.
    (4.8 x 17.1 x 9.3 cm)
Samuel H. Kress Collection
1957.14.86

PAGE 21
Paduan, 16th century
A Frog, early 16th century
Bronze sculpture, 2$\frac{3}{4}$ x 5$\frac{3}{4}$ x 3$\frac{1}{16}$ in.
    (7 x 14.6 x 7.7 cm)
Samuel H. Kress Collection
1957.14.92.(SC)

PAGE 23
American, 19th century
Birds, c. 1840
Oil on canvas, 17 x 14 in. (43.1 x 35.5 cm)
Gift of Edgar William and Bernice Chrysler Garbisch
1978.80.12

PAGES 24–25
Winslow Homer, American, 1836–1910
Right and Left, 1909
Oil on canvas, 28$\frac{1}{4}$ x 48$\frac{3}{8}$ in. (71.8 x 122.9 cm)
Gift of the Avalon Foundation
1951.8.1.(PA)

PAGE 26
Titian, Venetian, c. 1488–1576
Study of an Eagle, c. 1515
Pen and brown ink on laid paper, 3¹¹⁄₁₆ x 3⁷⁄₈ in.
   (9.4 x 9.3 cm)
Gift of J. Carter Brown
1991.62.1.(GD)

PAGE 27
Andrea Mantegna, Paduan, 1431–1506
Bird Perched on a Branch with Fruit, c. 1495
Pen and brown ink on laid paper, 4⅛ x 4½ in.
   (10.4 x 11.5 cm)
Andrew W. Mellon Fund
1976.33.1.(DR)

PAGE 29
Martin Johnson Heade, American, 1819–1904
Cattleya Orchid and Three Brazilian Hummingbirds, 1871
Oil on wood, 13¾ x 18 in. (34.8 x 45.6 cm)
Gift of The Morris and Gwendolyn Cafritz
   Foundation
1982.73.1.(PA)

PAGE 31
François Boucher, French, 1703–1770
Venus Consoling Love, 1751
Oil on canvas, 42⅛ x 33⅜ in. (107 x 84.8 cm)
Chester Dale Collection
1943.7.2.(PA)

PAGES 32 AND 33
Bernardino Luini, Milanese, c. 1480–1532
Procris and the Unicorn, c. 1520/1522
Oil, transferred from fresco to canvas, 90 x 42½ in.
   (228.6 x 108 cm)
Samuel H. Kress Collection
1943.4.60.(PA)

PAGE 35
Albrecht Dürer
St. Eustace, c. 1500/1501
Engraving, 13¹⁵⁄₁₆ x 10¼ in. (35.4 x 26.1 cm)
Gift of Robert Rosenwald
1971.15.1

PAGE 37
Dosso Dossi, Ferrarese, active 1512–1542
Circe and Her Lovers in a Landscape, c. 1525
Oil on canvas, 39⅝ x 53½ in. (100.8 x 136.1 cm)
Samuel H. Kress Collection
1943.4.49.(PA)

PAGE 39
Hans Hoffmann, German, c. 1530–1591/1592
Red Squirrel, 1578
Watercolor heightened with white and gold on
   vellum, 9⅞ x 7 in. (25 x 17.8 cm)
Woodner Family Collection
1991.182.5.(DR)

PAGES 40–41
John James Audubon, American, 1785–1851
Arctic Hare, c. 1841
Pen and black ink and graphite with watercolor and
   oil on paper, 24 x 34¼ in. (61 x 86.9 cm)
Gift of E. J. L. Hallstrom
1951.9.10

PAGE 43
Agnes Miller Parker, Scottish, 1895–
Fox, 1940
Wood engraving
Rosenwald Collection
1943.3.6713.(PR)

PAGES 44–45
D. G. Stouter, American, active in or after 1854
On Point, in or after 1854
Oil on canvas, 18¼ x 21¼ in. (46.3 x 52 cm)
Courtesy Gwynne Garbisch McDevitt. Gift of Edgar
   William and Bernice Chrysler Garbisch
1980.62.68

PAGE 47
Joseph Anderson Faris, American, 1833–1909
The Neigh of an Iron Horse, 1860s
Oil on canvas, 13⅞ x 17⅞ in. (35.1 x 45.4 cm)
Courtesy of Gwynne Garbisch McDevitt. Gift of
   Edgar William and Bernice Chrysler Garbisch
1980.62.69

PAGES 48–49
John Marin, American, 1870–1953
Sketch of Two Bison, c. 1950
Oil on canvas mounted on board, 5⅜ x 11¹⁄₁₆ in.
   (13.6 x 28.1 cm)
Gift of John Marin, Jr.
1986.54.10

PAGES 50–51
American, 19th century
Spring on the Range, last quarter 19th century
Oil on canvas, 21⅛ x 29⁵⁄₁₆ in. (53.7 x 74.5 cm)
Gift of Edgar William and Bernice Chrysler Garbisch
1971.83.14

PAGE 53 AND 54–55
John Constable, British, 1776–1837
Wivenhoe Park, Essex, 1816
Oil on canvas, 22⅛ x 39⅞ in. (56.1 x 101.2 cm)
Widener Collection
1942.9.10.(PA)

PAGE 56
H. Call, American, active 1876
Prize Bull, 1876
Oil on canvas, 19¹⁵⁄₁₆ x 24¹³⁄₁₆ in. (50.7 x 63 cm)
Gift of Edgar William and Bernice Chrysler Garbisch
1980.62.3.(PA)

PAGE 58
Albrecht Dürer
The Prodigal Son, c. 1496
Engraving, 9¾ x 3¹⁵⁄₁₆ in. (24.8 x 10 cm)
Rosenwald Collection
1943.3.3459.(GR)

PAGE 59
Martin Schongauer, German, c. 1450–1491
Family of Pigs, c. 1480/1490
Engraving, 2⅝ x 3¹¹⁄₁₆ in. (6.6 x 9.4 cm)
Rosenwald Collection
1943.3.79

101

Text Credits

PAGE 91
Sturtevant J. Hamblin, American, active c. 1845
Little Girl with Pet Rabbit, c. 1845
Oil on cardboard, 12⅛ x 9⅝ in. (30.8 x 24.5 cm)
Gift of Edgar William and Bernice Chrysler Garbisch
1953.5.70

PAGE 92
Edouard Manet, French, 1832–1883
A King Charles Spaniel, c. 1866
Oil on canvas, 18¼ x 15 in. (46.4 x 38.2 cm)
Ailsa Mellon Bruce Collection
1970.17.36

PAGE 93
Mary Cassatt, American, 1844–1926
Little Girl in a Blue Armchair, 1878
Oil on canvas, 35¼ x 51⅛ in. (89.5 x 129.8 cm)
Collection of Mr. and Mrs. Paul Mellon
1983.1.18.(PA)

PAGES 95 AND 96–97
Edward Hopper, American, 1882–1967
Cape Cod Evening, 1939
Oil on canvas, 30¼ x 40¼ in. (76.8 x 102.2 cm)
John Hay Whitney Collection
1982.76.6.(PA)

PAGES 98–99
Edward Hicks, *Peaceable Kingdom*
(see description for BAS-TITLE)

DESIGNED BY SUSAN MARSH ✧ COMPOSITION IN MONOTYPE DANTE BY DIX ✧ PRINTED AND BOUND BY AMILCARE PIZZI, MILAN, ITALY